BARBIE UNBOUND

A Parody of the Barbie Obsession*

Sarah Strohmeyer
Photos by Geoff Hansen

BARBIE UNBOUND

A Parody of the Barbie Obsession*

Sarah Strohmeyer
Photos by Geoff Hansen

*For Grownups

Published by New Victoria Publishers Inc., a feminist, literary, and cultural organization, PO Box 27, Norwich, VT 05055-0027.

Printed in Canada

Photos © Copyright 1997 by Geoffrey M. Hansen
1 2 3 4 5 6   20001   2000 1999 1998 1997

Library of Congress Cataloging-in-Publication Data

Strohmeyer, Sarah.
    Barbie unbound : A parody of the barbie obsession/ by Sarah Strohmeyer ; photos by Geoffrey M. Hansen.
        p.m.   cm.
    ISBN 0-934678-89-8
      1. Barbie dolls--Humor. 2. Dolls--Humor.   I. Hansen, Geoffrey M.
  II. Titles.
  PN6231.B324S77   1997
  818' .5407--dc21

                                                       97-19544
                                                        CIP

Table of Contents

Section I: From Tropical to Topical

Section II: From Hysterical to Historical

INTRODUCTION

You can't escape her.

Maybe as a grownup you thought you could. You thought Barbie would disappear, just like your pimples did. Perhaps you figured, never again will I have to catch her staring with that "Jeepers-you're-fat" look on her face. Because, compared to Barbie, of course you are.

Remember that foolish fit of youthful naiveté when you swore before all your hairy-legged classmates in Women's Lit that there would be a Barbie ban in your home? No daughter of yours would ever manipulate the manifestation of society's limitations on women. Ha!

Look around you. Barbie's lining store shelves. She's selling for fifty dollars a pop as a "nostalgia icon." She's more popular than ever.

And she's got no shame. Baywatch Barbie, Foam and Color Barbie, Totally Hair Barbie. She's practically screaming from the hot pink boxes, "I''m an idiot! All women are idiots. Brush you hair. Tease it. Color it, 'cause that's the only fun you're going to get in life."

Gasp, look down, your little Amelia's holding one in her pudgy hand right now. It's Great Date Barbie, a perfect symbol of fertile female sacrifice on the phallic altar of Prom Night. How did that happen? How did Amelia, who's been given nothing but gender-neutral Lincoln Logs and educational Discovery toys get hold of that?

The answer is you failed. You failed, you failed, you failed. And if you don't do something to rectify your dangerous mistake now, little Amelia will, as you very much feared, reach old age remembering high school as the very best time of her life.

Perhaps it's time to take a different tack. Fact is, Barbie is made up of indestructible plastic and she's going to be around long after your principles have been lost on the next generation. So, if you're going to coexist in the world with her, isn't it time you took the upper hand and got Barbie on your side? Forget *Kissing Barbie, Groupie Barbie, and Stewardess Barbie.* How about giving her some challenges—and outfits—to teach little Amelia about the lives of real women?

You've deconstructed her, now reconstruct her. Through this subversive guide, any parent can turn Barbie into the ultimate little feminist.

At a quiet moment, preferably when little Amelia is asleep, take *Great Date Barbie*, strip her bare. What do you have in your hand? An eleven and one-half inch doll, you say. A disproportionate miniature of male erotic projections. A symbol to be despised by all full-hipped, living and breathing females.

Hardly. Look again.

Barbie Unbound is here to the rescue. After nearly forty years in her pink plastic prison she is on parole, exploring the roles REAL women have assumed for years. And, with this guide, she will take you with her. She knows you detest the endless materialism, eternal youth and Cinderella lifestyle some feminists claim her previous persona promised her young playmates. Now, tiptoeing in the footsteps of some of the twentieth century's most notorious repenters—Robert S. McNamara, Lee Atwater and Tammy Faye Bakker among them—Barbie Unbound offers real life goals plus instructions on how to achieve them. Finding the necessary Barbie models this guide suggests might require some ingenuity—certainly Mattel wouldn't market these. Nevertheless we are confident that with a little tinkering you, and perhaps even your Barbie-obsessed daughter, will come to see the Pink Princess not as the enemy, but as the ultimate feminist teaching tool.

SECTION I:
FROM TROPICAL TO TOPICAL

OVERWEIGHT OUTCAST
ADOLESCENT BARBIE

Goal: To die young and leave an emaciated corpse that still looks too fat in jeans.

What You Will Need:

Wallflower Barbie, Prom Queen Barbie's "Big-Boned" Lockermate—Comes with three styles of unflattering, polyester gym uniforms, great personality and magic phone that never rings!

A Tiny Barbie for Barbie—For childhood inculcation of Barbie's materialistic and superficial values resulting in unattainable teenage fantasies.

Too-Cool Kens—Perfect for bashing unattainable teenage fantasies resulting from childhood inculcation of Barbie's materialistic and superficial values.

Background: When you think of Barbie several words might come to mind: tall, blonde, bimbo, she of the grotesquely distorted legs, waist and breasts. Concentration camp victim on silicone. But Barbie has not always elicited such pleasant images.

No, believe it or not, Barbie was once an overweight teenager, tipping the scales at twice her current weight. If you don't believe us, just get hold of some pictures of her from junior high school. What a cow! Which is exactly what the Kens used to yell at her as she lumbered down the school hallways.

"Hey, it's Barbie the Barbarian," the Cool Kens shouted. "Hope you don't eat us, too."

The Midges, Francies and Skippers weren't much nicer. Especially the cheerleader models. "I don't want her on my team," they whispered in gym class. "Ick."

Poor Barbie. Her only friends seemed to be the trolls. "Why don't we hang out and just be ugly and fat together?" the mutated, green, bug-eyed creatures suggested. "We can watch Star Trek!"

But that wasn't enough. Staring into the mirror at night she wished over and over again for an ideal body that seemed impossible to obtain.

"How I wish I had an over-sized head with bleached blonde hair," she prayed. "And breasts that stood out like torpedoes. A waist that could wear bracelets and legs that were longer than my torso."

Well, thank goodness for the free marketplace of high school bathrooms because there Barbie found some magic pills that made it possible for her dreams to come true. You might know those pills as speed, Christmas trees, black beauties or guarantees of premature heart attacks. All Barbie knew was that she was thinner than ever and her eyes were as wide as saucers. As an added bonus, she found she never needed sleep again.

Of course Barbie couldn't pay attention in school very well after that, so her grades slipped to the point where college was became an impossibility. As did the task of doing simple addition in her head.

But you know what? That didn't matter one whit. With all the modeling contracts and marriage proposals from wealthy Kens, Barbie would be swimming in money except for the fact that she has so little body fat she can't even float in Jell-O. Which just goes to show you, it's true that you can never be too thin, unless you want to swim across the English Channel and who would want to do that anyway?

Instructions: Holding Barbie's emaciated body in your left hand, wrap her thighs, middle (but not her breasts!) and butt in Silly Putty so for the first time she has the normal proportions of a 5'11" woman. Amazing, isn't it? Now take Mom's magnifying mirror and hold it up to Barbie so she can see her new image. Do this while attempting to squeeeeze Barbie into her favorite Size 3 swimsuit, preferably under fluorescent lights in a communal changing room. For added fun, have Midge whisper behind her back.

Discussion Questions:

1) In the forty years that Barbie has been around, Mattel has responded to cultural sensitivities by manufacturing Barbies of different ethnic groups, skin color and even physical abilities. The only model the company seems to have overlooked is one of different body proportions. Discuss this oversight in light of recent sexual discrimination lawsuits (keyword: stewardess).

2) Great Date Ken promised Overweight Outcast Adolescent Barbie he would take her to the prom—that was until Prom Queen Barbie's date, Not-So Great Date Ken, couldn't make it because his head popped off from having too much air inside. Now Great Date Ken wants to come to Prom Queen Barbie's rescue. How should Overweight Outcast Adolescent Outcast Barbie reply when Great Date Ken gives her the boot.
    a) "Sure, that's fine, and here's a preventative dose of penicillin for the dance."
    b) "Sure, that's fine, but how will you drive there without a working knee cap?"
    c) "Oh, so you're the one she picked for her Carrie reenactment. Congratulations!"

TEENAGE PREGNANT BARBIE

Goal: To find out what you're missing that *everyone else* is doing but that all the adults say you're not—or shouldn't be.

What You Will Need:

Growing-up Skipper—You're telling us!

Hormonally-Overcharged Ken—Who, him? What'd he do? He didn't touch her, he swears.

Not Barbie clothes—Ever take a look at those waists?

A lack of direction, a lack of self-esteem, how about just a lack of condoms.

Background: For years Barbie unknowingly dressed for sex. Skimpy skirts, skin-tight tops, mouth-watering bikinis. She wore them everywhere. The Barbie grocery store, the post office, even to her summer job at the Barbie Sweet Shop. Barbie thought she was just being hip and fashionable, but Hormonally-Overcharged Ken thought otherwise.

"Pant," he drooled.

But Barbie, being a good girl, didn't quite know what Ken was after. When she asked her creators at Mattel to explain, they said prim things like, "Barbies don't have sex" or " Our Barbies can't get pregnant." They told her just to keep her legs together. Hey, like what other choice did she have?

So Barbie didn't think twice when Ken asked her to spend the night in the Country Camper, although he couldn't be found after she started feeling sick a few weeks later. Maybe he was hiding under the couch? Meanwhile, the American Girls dolls started pointing their pudgy plastic fingers at her.

"That's what you get for parading around in those clothes," sniffed Felicity Merriman. "Twentieth century slut."

It was as though Hormonally-Overcharged Ken hadn't had any part in it at all!

"I was out driving in the Mustang with the guys," he told everyone. "Barbie who?"

Lucky for Barbie, she has corporate support which successfully passes off Barbie and Ken's mistake as "Baby Sister Kelly." Too bad the 500,000 teenage girls who get pregnant every year don't have marketing departments too.

Instructions: Dress Barbie in any outfit made by Mattel. Keep her ignorant. Introduce Ken. Wait for results.

Discussion questions:

1) Was Ken lying when he said he was out with the guys or does the fact that he doesn't possess a penis acquit him of Teenage Pregnant Barbie's charge? (For more on immaculate conception, see Blessed Barbie: She's Divine).

2) In 1963, Barbie creator Ruth Handler proclaimed that Barbie would never get pregnant. In response to girls' desire for a maternal Barbie doll, she issued "Barbie Babysits" which came with three books—*How to Get a Raise, How to Lose Weight (Don't Eat!)* and *How to Travel.* Say, you didn't know books would keep you from getting pregnant, did you?

LET'S GO NAVY! BARBIE GETS HER TAIL HOOKED

Goal: To enjoy the camaraderie that comes from being all you can be, especially if you be drunk off your ass.

What You Will Need:

She Asked For It Barbie—What did she expect after forty years of showing her legs like that.

Military Brat Ken—Give him a bottle and he drinks and wets, too!

A recent Gulf War, five-hundred Gulf War veterans, an open bar.

A gauntlet

Background: Lieutenant Barbie Coughlin was proud to be a member of the U.S. Navy. It had been tough at first—proving that she could do everything a boy could do—and better. But with her usually cheery attitude and go get 'em spirit, she was confident of success. Eventually she knew her hard work had paid off when her fellow officers embraced her with enthusiasm at the 1991 Tailhook Convention—with perhaps, too much enthusiasm.

"Whooweee!" Barbie shouted as her colleagues hoisted her over their shoulders in the hallway of the Las Vegas Hilton "Boy, you guys must really like me. Say, has

anyone seen my underwear?"

"Let's shave her legs!" one of the Military Brat Kens shouted. And they carried her off to the Leg Shaving Suite which is now standard at most convention hotels.

The next day Barbie wondered about her comrades' tactile tactics. "Something tells me they weren't applauding my intellect and skill," she said rubbing her sore behind which had been applauded frequently the night before.

So brave Barbie Coughlin came forward to complain, only to find—surprise, surprise—that the military didn't take her very seriously.

"Was that a mini-skirt you were wearing?" the Pentagon investigators asked, their lower jaws dropping in shock. "Now how could these men have pulled down your underwear when Barbies don't wear underwear? And what about that leg shaving? Barbie doesn't need to shave her legs. Everyone knows that."

Poor Barbie Coughlin. Of the fifty or more junior officers accused of running around naked, or assaulting women or being too drunk to stand up, only one lost a job. And can you guess who that was? You got it—Barbie Coughlin.

"I hear things are fairer over in the Army side," she decided. "Maybe I'll do better at the Aberdeen Proving Ground."

Instructions: Take five-hundred members of the U.S. Navy and Air Force. Remove wives. Douse with scotch. Insert Barbie. Watch Secretary of the U.S. Navy lose his job.

Discussion Questions:

1) Find the hidden keyword which appears 10 times in the following sentence: The assaulting associates assembled en masse at the '91 Tailhook Association acted like asses when they crassly harassed the lasses.

2) Some military officers have complained of a "double standard" in the Tailhook controversy saying that while men may have been mauling, defrocking and raping women, there were plenty of women who were having sex, too. Define the difference between assault and sex. Considering those officers weren't able to do what you just did, ponder the dim prognosis of this country's military future.

GRUNGE BARBIE

Goal: Goal? Like, I'm not into goals. Or that whole success thing. Hey! Who drank my beer?

What You Will Need:

Gen-X Barbie—Comes with own set of miniature tracks. And they're not for trains, if you get our drift.

Periodically Depressed Ken—He's stupid *and* contagious.

Two tickets to Seattle—Have fun!

Two tickets back from Seattle—Hello reality!

Background: At first, Grunge Barbie didn't think of herself as representative of her Slacker Generation. She abstained from beer because it was too fattening, and coffee, she feared, would just make her more perky. As for heroin, no way. Once you stuck a needle in her, it was a bear to get out. One time we had to use pliers.

But most of all, Grunge Barbie detested the clothes. Flannel shirts! Ripped jeans! Combat boots! Why, it was enough to make any Barbie hide under her fluffy Sweet Dreams bed and shut the door.

But all that changed the day Grunge Barbie met Periodically Depressed Ken.

"I like you, Barbie," said Periodically Depressed Ken as he slumped against a wall and absentmindedly checked for dropped food in his sleeve. "You've got teen spirit."

Finally, thought Barbie, a man who's not intimidated by cheerleaders.

"In fact," continued Periodically Depressed Ken, "You might even like Nine Inch Nails. You should check them out."

Well, of course, Barbie was in heaven. Any man who appreciated a girl with a bouncy personality and a good manicure was a man worth curling her hair for. That was until Periodically Depressed Ken started talking about Alice in Chains. Grunge Barbie didn't know who she was or why Periodically Depressed Ken was buying her gaudy jewelry, but Grunge Barbie figured it was time to make like a Barbie hair dryer and blow. When she summoned up enough courage to break up with him, Periodically Depressed Ken was visibly upset.

"Whatever," he said. And then he went back to work, searching the dumpster for old cigarette butts.

Instructions: Instructions? How dare you tell me what to do. Why, for eighteen years you parked me in front of the TV while you pursued your careers and money and stock options. Well, guess what, I'm not buying into your Eighties capitalistic crap. I'm gonna do what I want to do when I want to do it. You can just take your liberal, baby-boomer instructions and shove them up your previously cocaine-ravaged nose.

Discussion Questions:

1) Grunge Barbie has been invited to Directionless Midge's wedding in Seattle. (Barbie is so grunge she doesn't even care that Midge is getting married first). If the trip to Seattle from Barbie's home town of SunnyAllDay, Calif. is 1,100 miles, how many rides will Grunge Barbie have to hitchhike if each ride carries her essentially 64 miles? Considering that Grunge Barbie is traveling with her sister, Morphine, what are the chances Hitchhiking Grunge Barbie will actually make it to Directionless Midge's wedding alive?

2) Baby boomers worry that their children will be the first American generation to be worse off economically than their parents. Explain why their concern is valid or invalid in light of the fact that the generation before baby boomers has actually been borrowing heavily from the boomers' income to subsidize their social security payments—a debt that in all likelihood will not be repaid.

SAFE SEX BARBIE

Goal: To explore the consequences of forty years of unprotected sex.

What You Will Need:

Totally Hair Barbie—Like you'd even consider any other

Questionable-Sexuality Ken—(May substitute another Ken for Barbie for truly high risk adventure)

A condom—out of the package, please

Barbie Mini-Van, Corvette, parents' bed or any other place where unprotected sex is likely to occur.

Background: It used to be that Barbie and Ken would be satisfied with the simple pleasures of laying plastic hands side by side or a quick peck at the door of the Barbie Dream House. But Barbie was created before the mass distribution of birth control pills and since then a lot has changed. After Sun Lovin' Malibu Barbie (that slut) it seems Ken wasn't happy unless there was some plastic on plastic at the end of the evening. Poor Barbie—it was either put out or spend those Saturday nights with Midge.

Plus, there was always that nagging question in the back of her mind about Ken.

21

Maybe he was too perfect to waste those biceps on the softer sex. And how come he was so concerned with his tan and what about those clothes? Matching faux leather loafers and briefcase, please! But when she confronted him about his experimentation in the seventies, Ken was mum. He just lay there with that stupid grin on his face.

By the time AIDS came along, Barbie was seriously concerned. And she took action. She lay down the line with Ken—it was either safe sex or no sex. And though Ken was mighty bummed—you wouldn't believe the places he had to go to find hot pink plastic condoms—he's come to accept the new lifestyle. Still, it would be nice, he sometimes muses, if he had a dick on which to wear them.

Instructions:

There's nothing here you haven't seen in sex ed, or worse, young lady, but that's not our business. First undress Barbie and Ken, which should be a reflex action by now. Go into your father's upper left hand sock drawer. Remove condom. Remember to ask Dad why he has condoms anyway since you thought he had a vasectomy after you were born. Make Barbie and Ken kiss. Then, when the moment's right, carefully unroll condom over Ken. Lay them side by side. Not much fun, is it?

Discussion questions:

1) How do you suppose Barbie had a heart-to-heart discussion about safe sex with Ken when neither can move his or her lips?

2) Do you think Barbie's chances of avoiding unprotected sex would increase if she started wearing a bra? How about underwear?

3) Ken says he doesn't like wearing a condom. It's uncomfortable, plus he can't see. Do you think that's fair?

4) If sleeping with someone means you have, in a biological sense, slept with everyone that person has ever had sex with, then how many people has Barbie slept with if she's been dating an assortment of Kens for forty years. After thinking about it, do you think this is an appropriate doll to play with at your age?

PMS BARBIE

Goal: I have a goal, don't you worry. God, do you have to leave your underwear on the floor like that? All I do is pick up, pick up, pick up.

What You Will Need:

Bloated Barbie—It's water weight, mind your own business.

Annoying Ken—Says "I'm sorry" repeatedly but still can't get a break.

Chocolate bars, truck loads of salt

A white male medical establishment—Of course they don't understand, how could they—they're MEN!

Background: Barbie has always prided herself on being a cheerful team player, every day of every month, twelve months of the year, year after year. Why shouldn't she be? As a 6' 9" woman weighing 100 lbs, Barbie's body fat is essentially zilch. And that means not only does she have an over-extended body that has no chance of floating, but she can't menstruate either.

"Of course not," said Barbie. "Bleed? Ick"

But then the feminists attacked Barbie like piranha on dogmeat and in response Mattel produced a Barbie model that included the necessary seventeen to twenty-two percent body fat. Big mistake.

For twenty-six days in a month Barbie was fine. But one day she had trouble

zipping up her skirt.

"Damn," she thought. "Maybe it was those two bowls of popcorn I ate last night. Or perhaps it was the gallon of chocolate sauce I drank like water."

Going to work didn't make things any easier. As a model and stewardess she was supposed to be together and upbeat. Usually that was a snap, but not today.

"Why don't you try smiling for four hours," she snapped at the photographer.

"Ask for another bag of peanuts and I'll personally shove them—" she growled at a befuddled airline passenger.

Liberated Midge intervened. She told Barbie to relax, but Barbie was starting to get a persistent ache in the back of her head and she had a disturbing notion to pop Midge square on the nose.

"It's only PMS," Midge explained. "Stay away from alcohol and coffee, try to get extra exercise and rest and you'll be fine."

"You mean it's not just my imagination?" an incredulous Barbie asked.

"No, silly," Midge replied. "That's just a little fabrication to keep women from pursuing powerful roles in society. That's why the male-dominated toy world created Barbies in the first place."

Oh, thought Barbie, that explains me.

Instructions:

Very carefully open the Barbie package. Don't say anything. Don't even look at her sideways. Just do as she asks and we'll all be fine.

Discussion Questions:

1) Men are quick to point out when a woman is a tad cranky because of PMS. There seems to be no end in their delight in teasing women about this temporary phenomenon. Yet occasional PMS seems to be the permanent state of many men, the type who anger easily, crave potato chips and want to be left alone. Can you name that syndrome?

2) Oh you can't, huh. Did you try the term "off-season?"

BARBIE BOSS FROM HELL

Goal: To reflect on the nurturing environment created by new women executives in the post women's-lib American period.

What You Will Need:

"1980s Barbie"—Comes with off-white Chanel-inspired suit, a small handbag, computer-rolodex.

Half-Hearted Union Rep Midge—Still fighting for your right to have tampon machines in the bathrooms, sister. As for more comp time and better benefits, umm, that may take a few years. She'll keep ya posted.

A glass ceiling—Watch your head!

A lackey—Take a look in the Barbie mirror, sweetie.

Background: Barbie's had a lot of careers since her first days as an airline hostess. She's been a fashion model, babysitter, disco dancer, and even an astronaut. All without a lick of education. So it was only a matter of time before Mattel issued its "Great Careers" line and Barbie was pushed up the corporate ladder to become the under-qualified, under-educated executive boss many of us have come to know. And she has the purple-plastic attache to prove it.

At first, there was a honeymoon period. Barbie kept pretty quiet behind office doors, emerging only to freshen her make-up or sharpen a pencil.

Then things changed. Workers were ordered to work longer hours and take shorter lunches. When one explained she had to leave to tend to sick children, Barbie became so irate that she nearly kicked over the pink executive desk.

"I don't have kids and neither should you if you plan on moving up in this company," she snapped as she placed her hands on her tiny barren hips. "And don't forget to always smile, like me. I want happy workers. Happy, happy, happy."

There were other changes, some of which flopped. When Barbie instituted a dress code that modeled her fashion tastes, worker productivity declined 50%. It took female employees half an hour just to sit down so their skin-tight skirts didn't rip, and men had such a hard time learning how to walk on stiletto heels that three fell down the stairs and had to receive workers compensation. It was a disaster.

After that fiasco, Barbie rightly lost her job. Now she's much happier being chairman of the board.

Instructions: Dress Barbie in appropriate executive wear. The pink-polyester open suit coat etched in black works just fine. Holding Barbie in left hand, lie on floor with your arm outstretched above you. Now slowly bring Barbie down toward your face, closer, closer. Scary, isn't it? How'd you like to report to that each morning?

Discussion Questions:

1) It's time for your annual review. Barbie says you've done a fine job and gives you a two percent pay raise. Meanwhile, you and your colleagues do your own review of Barbie and find her performance is the pits. Yet she receives a bonus package equal to three times your salary. Just what are you doing wrong?

2) What things will get you further in the corporate world?

Education	Ignorance
Hard work	Major butt kissing
New ideas	Stealing someone else's new ideas
Coming early to work	Staying out late with the boss
Being a woman.	Being a man, even if you have to fake it

BARBIE LEE GIFFORD VISITS HER VERY OWN SWEATSHOP

Goal: To shake the invisible hand of capitalism that inconceivably rewards celebrities for campaigning against the cheap labor practices from which they previously made millions.

What You Will Need:

Talking Barbie Lee—Says "Look at Me! Look at Me! Look at Me!' Batteries never wear out.

Hit-in-the-head-too-many-times Football Star Ken Gifford—Comes pre-programmed for immovable action fun.

Adorable blonde children—for trotting out

Malnourished dark children—for sewing hems

Background: As a grown-up doll, Barbie Lee Gifford had achieved everything any Barbie ever wanted—a title in a junior miss pageant, a degree from a right-wing, teetotalling university, and the opportunity to work with The Goddess of Barbies, Miss Anita Bryant. She even got to be on television and issue her own line of clothing—Barbie Lee's "I Wouldn't" wear. No wonder she was so perky. Too bad you can't be more cheerful like Barbie Lee.

But despite the fact that her "I Wouldn't" wear retailed at end-of-sale prices, it never occurred to Barbie Lee to wonder why her clothes were so cheap.

"I don't know," she mused in the gourmet kitchen of her seven-bedroom Connecticut estate. "It must be elves."

And in fact the Barbie Lee clothes *were* made by elves. Little, teeny-tiny Honduran elves to be exact. And they weren't the only ones. There were little elves in China and Taiwan and Singapore and even elves hidden just a few blocks from Barbie Lee's television studio in the good old U.S. of A., too.

And because these elves were so small and one might say, insignificant, they didn't cost much to feed and clothe. Why, they could work 20 hours a day and be paid just thirty-five cents an hour. They must be magic!

Then one day some grumpy old union organizers ruined all the fun. They said elves didn't exist. They said elves were real people and should be paid living wages.

The next day Barbie Lee sent her husband downtown to pay the little elves $12 each. "Whew, glad we fixed that," they said over a well-deserved bottle of Cristal that night.

But Barbie Lee can't be blamed for such human rights violations. "I don't think I should be held responsible for anything I don't know about," she said on national television.

Hmm, we'll need a moment to think that one over, Barbie Lee. In the meantime, you'd better check the toilet because we think you left your career there.

Instructions: Get on the bus. Get off the bus. Get to work. I don't care if it's 110 degrees in here. You've got ten minutes to have that baby and then back to the Singer! Est necessisto to speedupo your producion, si! I've got a job in the sugar cane fields for you if you don't shape up, you know.

Discussion Questions:

1) Barbie Lee says that after her experience with the Honduran sweatshops she knows all about medieval working conditions in the Third World. And as spokeswoman for a cruise line, she knows all about boat people. Discuss.

2) Math Quiz: Four Barbie outfits take three hours to make and retail for $6.50. Subtracting corporate profits and overhead costs along with the costs of distribution and retail sales, how much money is left over to pay the overseas laborer who actually sewed those outfits?

PRO-LIFE BARBIE VS. PRO-CHOICE MIDGE

"It's a Barbie, Not a Choice!" OR "If You Don't Believe in a Barbie, Don't Have One"

Goal: Familiarize yourself with both sides of the highly controversial abortion issue while turning your ho-hum apolitical Barbies into action-packed "Rock `em, Sock `em Activist Robots."

What You Will Need:

    Pro-Choice Midge**—She's right.

    Pro-Life Barbie**—No, she's right.

    Supreme Court Justices—You need just five.

      Warning—Both dolls are highly volatile and subject to unpredictable explosions.

Background: It used to be that Pro-Life Barbie and Pro-Choice Midge were the best of friends. Sure, Pro-Choice Midge was homelier but that was okay. Nothing, not even deep-seated jealousies, could come between such good pals. Then the U.S. Supreme Court handed down a decision in 1973 called Roe V. Wade and it legalized abortion. Pro-Life Barbie thought it was an icky ruling—how could people do that to Barbies before they were even out of the box!

36

But Pro-Choice Midge didn't feel quite the same way. She felt as though a great weight had been lifted off her shoulders—and it wasn't the carrying case that had just been knocked down on top of her. No, she felt liberated. For the first time, she realized, she wasn't trapped by her manufactured destiny. Why, she nearly shouted, she didn't have to have a Barbie if she didn't want to!

Unfortunately, Pro-Life Barbie and Pro-Choice Midge couldn't get along after that. Pro-Life Barbie thought Pro-Choice Midge was a heartless doll motivated by selfish ambitions that were antithetical to Barbie's deeply ingrained values of home, car and frequent change of clothes. Pro-Choice Midge thought Pro-Life Barbie was a brainless automaton who only spouted words she had been programmed to say. Well, that part was true, both had to admit, but still!

Instructions:

Change the subject.

Discussion Questions: (Hint: Some have no correct answers)

1) If Pro-Choice Midge is against the death penalty, how can she be for abortion?

2) Pro-Choice Midge's nylon neon-blue top and hip-huggin' yellow slacks are usually appropriate apparel for picnics, protests and other outdoor events. How come they won't work for the weekly Saturday morning pro-choice demonstration outside the abortion clinic? (Hint: consider bulk of bullet-proof vest.)

3) Where does Pro-Life Barbie get the right to mandate that others continue pregnancies when she will never have to be pregnant herself? (Try this one on Ken, too.)

VIRGINIA SLIMS BARBIE DATES TOBACCO LAWYER KEN

Goal: Unveil the weight-loss secret shared by millions of women—some of whom are still alive!

What You Will Need:

    Fashion Photo Barbie—For objectification in male gaze

    Talking Stacy—Older models may need new voice box.

    Tobacco Lawyer Ken—Soul not included.

    146,000 tiny Barbie cigarettes—To support a twenty-year, pack-a-day habit.

Background: Modeling swimsuits and underwear-revealing skirts has always kept Barbie's diet and exercise regimen on target. But one day she discovered that her steady weight of three ounces was no longer acceptable on the runway. The message was clear—lose the weight or retire to the box.

"I don't eat anything at all and still I can't lose weight," Barbie moaned one day to her friends Stacy, Francie and Skipper—whose flat chest even Barbie eyed with

envy these days.

Then Talking Stacy let Barbie in on a little secret shared by models everywhere. "Have you tried cigarettes?" she asked, handing Barbie a teeny-tiny pack.

Barbie lit one up. At first it was awkward; she couldn't fit the cigarette between her molded fingers and not being able to open her mouth made smoking difficult. Fortunately, her body adjusted and in no time Barbie was lighting up with all the ease of a high school teacher.

Best of all, the unwanted plastic virtually melted off her body.

Clean Cut Ken didn't like it. "You've lost that new-car plastic smell," he said one day. "And your hair is singed."

That bothered Barbie and she tried to quit. But she found stopping cold turkey made her so cranky that she kicked Clean Cut Ken out of the Barbie Sweet Slumbers bed, especially after he pointed out that she was developing a couple of love handles.

"What am I going to do?" she cried over a tiny Barbie beer one evening.

"Keep smoking," said a well-dressed Tobacco Lawyer Ken who whipped out a $100 bill to wipe her tears. "It's your constitutional right. It's an informed adult choice. Best of all, it's good for you. Say, my colleagues over at Philip Morris are having a little get-together, want to join me?"

"Usually, I would," she replied, curiously studying the top of his head. "But, to tell you the truth, you look a little horny."

Instructions: Take one of your parents' cigarettes apart. Cut the paper to tiny doll size and sprinkle tobacco down the center. Now carefully roll it up. If you can't get the hang of it, chalk it up as just another course in college preparation.

Discussion Questions:

1) Some critics might argue that smoking tarnishes Barbie's All-American image. But Southern Senators say a ban on cigarettes is un-American because it would put thousands of tobacco farmers out of work. How can Barbie win in this situation?

2) Barbie says she smokes because she looks cool and the weight stays off. But now Talking Barbie has a raspy voice, her mouth has burned away and doctors say she's not long for the landfill. When Barbie tried to turn around and sue the companies that make, advertise and profit from the product that did all this to her, a federal judge said no. Is that fair?

midge d. lang and BARBIE DEGENERES: A LOVE STORY

Goal: To conjure up an immediate gag order from Mattel just by whispering these magic words: Bulldyke Barbie.

What You Will Need:

Blonde Butch Barbie—Look in the closet.

Best Friend Midge—She's there, too, but lately she's been thinking of stepping out.

Great Date Ken—He's not that great. Maybe as a friend.

Background: For years Barbie DeGeneres and Great Date Ken went on dates that ended with nothing more than a kiss at the door. Ken found this frustrating but, oddly enough, Barbie DeGeneres didn't seem to mind.

"C'mon Barbie," Ken used to ask over and over again. "Let's just do it."

When Barbie DeGeneres finally agreed and so-called Great Date Ken dropped his trousers, it was all she could do to fake a little enthusiasm.

"Is that all there is?" she asked Deflated Date Ken when it was over. "It looks more exciting in the movies."

After that midge and Barbie started spending more and more time together. They became roommates and even vacationed in the sand box with other like-minded Barbies. On weekends they lay around naked on the back porch. It's not that they had anything against Ken, they decided, it was just that he had nothing to offer.

Meanwhile, Barbie DeGeneres wrestled with her inner feelings until, one day, she poured her heart out to midge d. lang.

"midge, I know 10 percent of Barbies are lesbians and that I'm one of them," she sobbed. "But if I let everyone know that, Mattel will throw me back in the closet. They'll accuse me of causing market losses and of being inappropriate for family viewing."

"Hmm," said midge as she thought about the official Barbie thigh-high stockings and purple see-through underwear. "Mattel's one to talk."

So Barbie DeGeneres and midge d. lang formulated a strategic plan. First, Barbie would leak rumors for months, then she would give interviews and finally she would go on talk shows. After that she would go public.

The reaction wasn't what they expected.

"We had our suspicions about you and midge all along," the Mattel Board of Directors said. "Fortunately for you, our marketing studies show there's a sizable niche for a gay doll."

Which just goes to show you that 14 million lesbian Barbies can't be wrong.

Instructions: Continue to play with Barbie and Midge as you always have. Admit it, you never really played with Ken anyway, except to dress him up in evening wear.

Discussion Question:

Which is more morally offensive—a "well-developed" doll that over stimulates a young girl's prepubescent sexual curiosity while closing her mind to alternative female images or a doll who prefers other dolls?

P.C. BARBIE GOES TO THE CO-OP

Goal: To find chemical-free, natural stuff that doesn't come from China.

What You Will Need:

Totally-Organic Barbie—Now one billionth the shelf-life of original Barbie!

Dolphin-free tuna

Pesticide-free espresso beans

Mildly-disturbing body odor

Background: Ever since her perfect plastic body popped from the mass-molds of Japan, Barbie has been happy to satisfy herself with the tiny foods she found at the Barbie Supermarket: plastic bananas, everlasting tomatoes, teeny-tiny bags of Ore-Ida French Fries and, best of all, Wonder Bread. It never occurred to Barbie to ask where they came from, who made them or what they were made of. Plastic. That was all she needed to know and that was fine with her.

But when Living Barbie (that flat-footed, musk-smelling hippie of the 1970s) told her that plastic was actually a petroleum-based product that had been linked with numerous types of cancers, Barbie was aghast.

"Cancer? Why, that could mean I might temporarily lose my hair," she thought,

Net Wt. 54 g (1.9 oz.)

T__sion Tamer

49

as far as her non-existent brain could think "Eeww."

And so P.C. Barbie took a trip to the local co-op. Hoping, as always, for fashion correctness, she abandoned the hot-pink bikini and high heels she usually donned for shopping and instead chose something from Barbie's Church Collection: an unbleached cotton peasant dress, hand-sewn Birkenstocks and Mexican silver jewelry (made by adequately-compensated craftsmen from a socialist-organized cooperative).

At the co-op Barbie met dolls she'd never even heard of before. Feminist Francie, whose Ken actually stayed home with the children, encouraged Barbie to consider a non-exploitative career outside of modeling. New Age Julia saw Barbie's pink plastic aura. Soon Barbie was letting her body hair grow, abandoning deodorant and using her breasts for something besides fulfilling Ken's expectations.

Some co-op workers were not as nice, though. Occasionally while stocking tofu Grateful Dead Groupie Gretta would remark that Barbie should turn herself into the recycling center. But Barbie knew that was just the hemp talking.

Instructions: Oh, instructing someone is so paternalistic. I mean, who am I from my Western, Euro-privileged background to tell you, someone obviously of a lesser spiritual plane, what to do? You know? Hey, you want some chamomile?

Discussion Questions:

1) Which is more egalitarian, a mass-produced doll that most parents can afford to purchase or an equivalently-priced pound of co-op coffee?

2) Can you find which item is out of place? A co-op, an Ivy League education, membership to the Democratic Party, a Saab 9000, a 1986 Ford Escort carrying six members of an illegal-immigrant family hoping to be fed for a month on $200 total.

WELFARE QUEEN BARBIE

Goal: To find a reason to get out of bed in the morning.

What You Will Need:

Bingo Barbie—Play with her every other Tuesday night at Our Lady of The Holy Roller.

PTSD (Post Traumatic Surfing Disorder Ken)—Do not disturb.

Doritos, Coke and bologna—for lunch.

Doritos, Coke, and bologna—for dinner.

Plain Coke—for breakfast (Welfare Queen Barbie's dieting tip).

Background: Destined-To-Be-Welfare-Queen Barbie had essentially two goals in life: to be queen of her high school prom and to marry Ken. Lucky for her, both dreams came true when she turned eighteen and Destined-To-Be-Welfare-Queen Barbie could relax knowing that, with Ken's salary as a surfing instructor, her future was secure.

But six months into the job, Ken was hit on the head with the surfboard and doomed to a life of collecting disability and making nuisance phone calls to local utility companies. Barbie, already the mother of Baby Sister Kelly, took a stab at close to fifty-seven careers, none of which she could hold for fifteen minutes before she

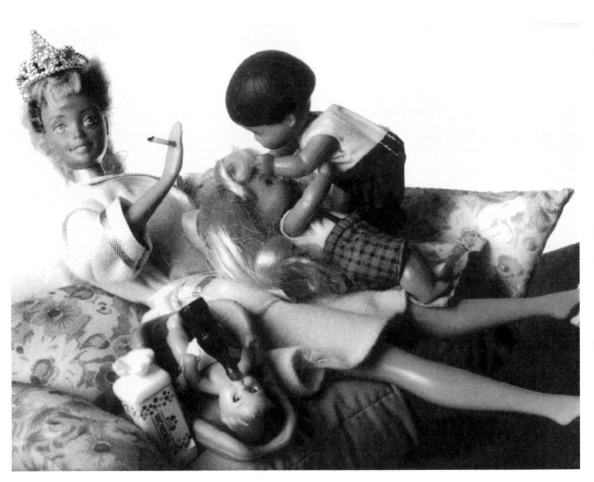

53

was tossed aside for other toys. With no more than a high school education, her options looked dim.

"Thank goodness for welfare," she sighed as she poured herself another Coke and lit a Lucky. "I couldn't work now anyway. Who'd look after my 13 Baby Sister Kellies?"

Of course the $418 a month she received for the entire family couldn't cover her budget for Barbie shoes, Welfare Queen Barbie had to admit. Before long, the Barbie Corvette was up on blocks, Welfare Queen Barbie's roots turned to black and the bank had put the Dream House up for auction.

About the only highlights in her life were the monthly conjugal visits with Ken in the Barbie Big House where he had been sentenced for forging Barbie's logo to competing products without Mattel's written permission. Although recently she'd gone off those visits, too.

"Not tonight, PTSD Ken," she said sourly. "I've heard rumors about you and Jailbird Joe."

It would seem Barbie was never meant to lead the life of leisure she assumed had been her destiny. Recently, a group of conservative lawmakers demanded that she seek employment through a new program called "workfare."

"Work? Fair?" asked Barbie, who had always done poorly at spelling. "I don't think so."

Instructions: Wake up. Feed the kids, dress them, now pile into the broken-down Chevy Impala. Take half to day care, a third to pre-school and the rest to the social workers. Fix the car. Beg to have the electricity turned back on. Aren't you ready to work yet? Oh, no, don't tell me another kid's sick again! How do you think you're ever going to learn how to play Barbie at this rate?

Discussion Questions:

1) Social worker Midge says that Welfare Queen Barbie needs to dress better in order to get better jobs. She has recommended two outfits from Barbie's "Unemployment" line. Which would you choose: the Pink Collar Party Dress (comes with own pink slip) or the "Mini" wage Skirt.

2) Now that PTSD Ken is out of jail, he is collecting disability payments again. If he has started moonlighting at a local loading dock run by a suspect organization, which will come first if his new employment is discovered by state authorities: his arrest on fraud charges or his rest at the bottom of the Barbie Splash 'N Fun Pool.

SHOCK JOCK BARBIE

Goal: To explore the medium once used by Edward R. Murrow to bring the world face to face with the bombing of London and now occupied by Howard Stern for an in-your-face bombardment of bad taste.

What You Will Need:

Private Parts Barbie—Guess what? Barbie doesn't have any private parts.

Always Chuckling Sidekick Ken—Aww, ha, ha, ha. Oh, you're bad. Hey, hey, now you're going too far. I can't believe I get paid for this. Schmucks.

Imaginary FCC regulators—To boost ratings.

Background: Being a totally visual personage, Barbie never considered a career in radio, even though she can't talk—a plus in some markets. But the whole world knew about Barbie and the fact that she liked to lie around naked and that was enough to get her a disc jockey job greeting New York commuters from 7 to 10 a.m.

"I have tits!" she screamed into the microphone. "And an ass, too! I'm even sitting on it right now."

She was an immediate hit.

"She said she has tits!" a commuting stock broker in his Chrysler LaBaron tit-

tered to himself. "And an ass, too." He sighed with satisfaction; his morning was made.

Well, the FCC, which regulates what words can be said over the airwaves, couldn't let that go on much longer.

"There are seven dirty words you can't say on radio and you just said at least one, we think," the stern regulators told Shock Jock Barbie. "And you didn't mention us once! Now we're really steamed."

But Shock Jock Barbie was confused. The naughty words she learned at Mattel didn't include tits or ass. To Barbie those were called assets. She knew some dirty words, though, and if it was dirty words her listeners wanted to hear, Shock Jock Barbie thought, well, then she'd give them an earful.

"I'm fat and wooden!" she screamed into the microphone. "And unmarketable and unsaleable. I'm unpopular!"

Needless to say, Shock Jock Barbie is now pursuing another line of work. Last we heard it was handing out tickets at a New Jersey tollbooth. Every once in a while, though, she gets fan mail, most of it from disgruntled employees at a company in El Segundo, California.

Instructions:

Place headphones on Barbie. Have her paint the breasts of the doll sitting next to her. Make her ask the other doll if she would like sex. An enema? How about details of her last IRS audit or the other dolls' sexually transmitted diseases. Good. You've just passed your first course and are on your way to an exciting career as a radio station manager. Congratulations!

Discussion Questions:

1) In her blockbuster bestseller, *I Wish I Had Private Parts,* Barbie Stern proudly boasts that she has always been faithful to her husband, Ken, even though she simulates sex under the console during broadcasts. Explain why this is the least relevant piece of information in your life next to the option on your IRS form to donate one dollar of your money so other people can run for a job that is more powerful and pays better than your own.

2) Who is better qualified to lead the "Morning Zoo"?

a) a recovering alcoholic chain smoker who specializes in getting the President or leaders of various Congressional committees to say "doo-doo" on the air.

b) a bloated, thrice-divorced Conservative who proclaims the virtues of submissive women and the tobacco industry.

c) a convicted felon who encourages militia groups to take over the government.

d) a mute doll with a pleasant demeanor and no political views whatsoever.

HOT FLASH BARBIE

Goal: To appreciate the wonderful benefits of aging that are to die for.

What You Will Need:

Baby-Boomer Barbie—So you thought you were immortal, did you?

Mid-Life Crisis Ken—Comes with all-terrain vehicle, ropes (for mountain climbing), Bungee cord, snowboard and proctologist.

A little Barbie-sized estrogen patch—For buying a little time.

Background: When Barbie heard that her fortieth anniversary was just around the corner, she was ecstatic.

"Forty years old," she thought, glancing admirably in the Barbie mirror. "And I don't look a day over 18. I am sooooo perfect."

But wait! What was that? Was that a gray hair? There wasn't just one, there were several. Soon Barbie noticed other disturbing signs as well. For one thing, she had started to let out a groan of relief whenever she sat down. For another, she couldn't keep the names of all the other Barbies straight.

"Hey, Holida…I mean, Malib…uhm Bed Time, no Bath Blast. Busy, yeah that's it, Busy Barbie, could you get me my cane?"

Hot Flash Barbie had also broken several bones. Those years in the modeling

61

business had taken their toll, after all. Late night parties, smoking, poor nutrition. Physically, Barbie was a mess. And Ken noticed.

"I have to work late at the office," he called to tell her one evening. "Something's come up."

"Guess what, Ken," suspicious Hot Flash Barbie snapped back. "You don't have an office."

That's right. Ken, who's been a surgeon, a construction worker, a Wall Street broker, a surfer, a Big Brother (what's the story on that one, by the way?), a logger, and, frankly, can't seem to hold a job to save his life, was now a bum. Except he didn't call it being a bum. He called it "early retirement."

"I need to get out of the rat race, to smell the flowers, to find my inner spear," he explained while flipping through sailing brochures.

"Yeah, yeah," said Hot Flash Barbie who had just put on a pair of shorts to go outside in the snow. "Turn down the heat. What's wrong with me?"

Well, ha, ha, there's nothing wrong with you, Barbie. Nothing that a little hair color, tummy tuck, face lift and estrogen can't cure. Say, you wouldn't be interested in some land in Florida, would you?

Instructions: Oh, not now. I'm too tired.

Discussion Questions:

1) Barbie was introduced in 1959, which means that her fortieth anniversary is just over a year away. So what's her real age now, considering that Mattel claims she was supposed to be about "18 to 24" in 1959?

2) After Barbie's assets started slipping, she underwent plastic surgery and now recommends it for everyone. That's easy for her to promote, though, considering she's plastic. How do you remold new breasts, waists, hips, thighs, necks and vaginas for women who are made out of flesh and bone?

3) How will Barbie know she's reached menopause if she's never had a uterus?

4) Plastic surgery should be easy for Barbie—after all she's plastic, but how about the rest of us?

BARBIE UNBOUND: THE INTERVIEW*

*This is a parody, of course. If you truly believe Barbie can speak, you've been playing with Barbie too long, don't you think?

SS. I understand that this has been a difficult, although exciting time, since publicly coming out as "unbound."

BU. I'll say. I mean, I never expected this reaction, this support. I just want to say, that I'm still the same old Barbie—the same Barbie doing more fulfilling things, maturing. Also, on the advice of my lawyers a couple of ground rules. First, I really can't discuss Mattel. I know there's been a lot of publicity in the business press about my relationship with them but the bottom line is I'm still under contract, so that's that, I guess. And another, that's Joe…

SS. You mean G.I. Joe?

BU. Yeah, him. Again, stuff's been leaked. So Joe and I agreed we wouldn't talk about our relationship publicly even though I'm hounded night and day by the tabloids. So that's got to be off limits, too.

SS. When did you start, shall we say, coming unbound?

BU. Oh, in the Seventies. It's been a long process and I guess it took me a little longer than most women. A lot of my friends were unbinding in the Sixties when I was still happy babysitting and trotting on the beach in high-heeled shoes. I wasn't experimenting with mind-altering substances or into that free love stuff, you know. My philosophy was you are what you eat and since I can't really eat anything, I was nothing.

Also, since my breasts stood out like rockets , I never wore a bra , so there was nothing to burn. Of course, Gloria and Jane tried to turn me on to women's lib and stuff, but I just wasn't ready to hear it.

SS. Gloria and Jane?

BU. Yeah, Gloria Steinem and Jane Fonda. We actually were great friends back in California in the early '60s, before the whole world started coming apart.

SS. Really?

BU. Sure, Gloria was writing *The Beach Book*—you know, this whole thing about how to dress at the beach to pick up men. And she was working at the Playboy Club nights while I was doing modeling. And Jane…what a party girl! She was shooting *Barbarella* and the bashes she threw! But, of course, that's before she got whacked out and went overseas. And I just want to say right now, to our men and women who served in Vietnam, that I had no part, no part whatsoever, in supporting her on that. I thought it was disgraceful, personally.

SS. But those women were unbound years ago. What finally moved you in their direction?

BU. Hmmm. Well, I guess you could say it was an accumulation of experience. I think after a while all the anti-Barbie editorial cartoons, artwork and columns started getting to me. I couldn't ignore it any more. Mattel was trying to shut them up—or respond, however you look at it—by giving me new roles—astronaut, pediatrician. But still, I was wearing these short skirts and ridiculously high heels and no one was being fooled.
 Then one day when we were moving I was accidentally packed away with some

texts from a mother's feminist literature class. English, Ehrenreich, Mulvey. I read them all. And I finally confronted my past. Let's face it, there's good reason to believe that I'm modeled on a postwar German pornographic doll., Lilli, which men used to hand out to their mistresses. It dawned on me that I'm nothing more than the ultimate female projection of men's desires.

SS But I'm confused. What does that have to do with this book?

BU. Well, you know, although I can't change—my feet will always be pointy, my face perpetually cheerful. my breasts will be like cement D-cups. But what I do can change. I don't have to wear head-to-toe pink. I don't have to pretend that there's nothing more to life than weddings and prancing down the runway. I can confront the tough issues —poverty, AIDS, underpaid immigrant labor—some of the best—and the worst— female role models. From Marie Curie to Marie Antoinette.

SS. Wow, that's some agenda. Does that mean you're abandoning the whole Barbie schtick? The Dream House, the Corvette, the supermarket?

BU. No, no. I've got to do something to pay for the carrying case, ha, ha. I'm still under contract with Mattel, so I'll be doing the old Barbie stuff as my day job. Being unbound is on my own time, something I do out of love.

SS. How does Ken feel about this?

BU. (*Pause*) That's a tough one. It's been…do you mind if I have a cigarette? I know I shouldn't but it's my last vice. I even gave up speed last month and, believe me, that was not easy.

Let's see, you asked me about Ken. Well, as you may have read, Ken and I have

had our ups and downs lately. Starting with a few years ago when he realized he was gay. And that got a lot of press—whoo boy. Of course we all knew it or suspected it for years. But we've been married probably forty billion times and his announcement has been quite an adjustment, although I must give credit to Ken right now. The courage he showed in coming out gave me the strength, and I mean this sincerely, to examine the possibility of my being unbound. So he's been very supportive.

SS. The irony, of course, is that you're kind of the symbol, the epitome of being bound. Starting with your feet…

BU. Yeah, the feet , the feet. God the feminists love the feet. They're always comparing it to historical attempts by men to control women's movement, you know like the, the, oh yeah, the Chinese with the bound feet. Mince, mince, mince. It's overblown, I think.

SS. Have you thought of surgery?

BU. No, I'm beyond that. I can't do anything about my feet or my face. So that's the way it stays. On the inside I may be contemplative, or angry, or crying or sympathetic, but on the outside I'll always look like I'm another soccer mom on Valium. But you know, one of the best things about being unbound is you just accept yourself for who you are. You just say, no looking back. From now on, I am who I am, warts and all.

SS. But you don't have any warts.

BU. Not yet. Say, I've really got to run. Send me a copy will ya. You're a doll.

SECTION II:

FROM HYSTERICAL TO HISTORICAL

BARBIE D'ARC

Goal: Learn about feminist will in the Dark Ages and about the effects of polyvinyl chloride incineration at the same time.*

What You Will Need:

Miraculous Barbie—She's incredible—at least to skeptics.

Sticks, stake, fire.

A group of hypocritical Roman Catholic accusers.

A Pope—For the future

A burning religious conviction or worrisome symptoms of acute onset schizophrenia.

Background: Known as the "Maid of Orleans," Barbie D'Arc was a teenage girl who could neither read nor write (just like today's Barbie) and who lived from 1412 to 1431. While other kids were chasing each other around the maypole or holding

*Note: See "What's My Melting Point: Barbie Becomes Acid Rain" for explanation as to why older Barbies caused acid rain and today's models do not (Good for you, Barbie!)

hands during the Saturday night bloodletting, Barbie d'Arc was sitting under trees listening to voices that told her to get out there and lead an army. And to look good doing it, too.

At first, it was hard convincing those men of her strategic cunning, even when she was wearing her most see-through chain mail. After witnessing her fine figure straddling a horse, they said, "Sure, you ride in front of us, we'll be right behind you." Barbie d'Arc's trim and athletic visage turned out to be so inspiring that she led them to victory over the British at the siege of Orleans in 1429. Whew! It was a lot tougher than beach fun volleyball and, boy, was that armor heavy!

Alas, all did not go well for Barbie d'Arc. She was seventeen and not getting any dates, despite being surrounded by men. And to make things worse, she was captured by some British-sympathizing French who placed her in jail and tried her as a witch. She was forced to wear ugly-brown, scratchy clothes and sit in a windowless cell. How she longed for the cotton-candy airiness of her Dream House.

When the guys suggested a bonfire, Barbie d'Arc was all game. Then she discovered they'd be roasting her. Oh well, Barbie d'Arc concluded in her ever optimistic way, at least they still think I'm hot.

Instructions: Get to the good part. Place Barbie in outfit, tie to stake, pile sticks at foot. Get your best friend to perform last rites as you light the match. Turn face upward. Pray that your parents don't catch you. Pray that a spark does not leap to your porch and set the house on fire.

Discussion Questions:

1) Do you think the band of accusers would have been more sympathetic to Barbie if she hadn't foolishly cut her hair so short?

2) What dress do you think she picked out after a hard day at battle? Did she make dinner for all the boys, too?

3) Do you think that the sexual frustration felt by the celibate priests was a factor in their decision to proclaim her a witch and order her execution? Or do you think they merely wanted to put on display male power and dominance over women in an agricultural and religiously oppressive society? If so, why?

GROOVIN' GRAVITY GALILEO BARBIE

Goal: To study Galileo's law of falling bodies and watch Barbie's chest blow apart after a five-story drop to concrete.

What You Will Need:

Your Friend's Barbie—Pick her favorite

Your friend's other expendable toys

A new friend

Background: Quick, what's the mathematical formula for velocity?

If your answer is "duh" and you're a girl, then according to the school psychologists, you suffer from "math anxiety." No, you're not stupid, lazy or anything else that kids who couldn't multiply and divide used to be called. You're just anxious. Guess what? You're anxious because you have low self-esteem. And do you know why you have low self esteem? Well, some know-it-all people (we call them feminists) think it's because you play with Barbies too much.

Impossible. No one can play with Barbies too much. And anyway, we can prove that playing with Barbies can teach you how to understand and remember the formula for velocity. Here goes.

Once there was a Greek mathematician named Aristotle who thought that

heavy things and light things fell at different speeds. Turned out he didn't know what he was talking about (and he never even saw a Barbie). He must have had a lot of anxiety, not to mention really low self-esteem.

Then, in the 16th century, a teenage guy (just like Ken!) named Galileo dropped stuff off the leaning tower of Pisa, although it wasn't leaning at the time, and proved that all things fall at the same speed. He found they fell at 32.16 feet per second per second which, in Barbie language, sounds like she just flipped out and forgot to stop saying "per second."

Now Barbie has always claimed she is immune to gravity, unlike your mother who has noticed her own body parts descending daily. Then again, you wouldn't drop your mother off a five-story building. Or would you?

Instructions:

Dress Barbie in her most colorful outfit (to look her best flying through the air). Lean out of the highest window you can find. (We are not liable if you have so much low self esteem that you fall.) Get your best friend to stand on the ground with a stop watch. Yell, Banzai! and release Barbie. See what happens to Barbie when she hits the pavement. Now see what happens when you try to drop a paperweight and Barbie at the same time. No, we didn't say drop the paperweight on that businessman walking by. Can your friend run really, really fast?

Discussion Questions:

1) How fast would it take Mr. Coach Testosterone, your physics teacher with the bad breath, to fall if you dropped him from the top of the school stadium if the wind were blowing at thirty-five knots? Do you think he would stop snickering when you raised your hand in class if you were able to run that experiment?

2) Why do you need to know physics anyway? That's for boys, isn't it?

IT RHYMES WITH BITCH:
BARBIE AT SALEM

Goal: To test if Barbie is pure evil or just another victim of poor marketing.

What You Will Need:

Puritanical Barbie—May come with Grace or not, you can never really know.

Hallucinating Skipper—Can find in any high school bathroom.

An homicidal reaction—Born from male fear of women's reproductive and intellectual powers amidst paternalistic religious systems.

A sense of humor—severely lacking in seventeenth century Massachusetts

Background: Goody Barbie was the most devout teenager in 1692 Massachusetts. She loved nothing more than to test her bendable legs by kneeling for hours on the ice-cold plank boards of the town church. And her ability to sit straighter longer than anyone during the seven-hour Sunday catechism was the envy of Salem.

Then funny things started to happen. Cows stopped giving milk and people had dreams of purple satin underclothing etched in black lace that really itched.

"It's Goody Barbie," hissed Goody Skipper, who had always been a little jealous of Goody Barbie's generous proportions. "She hath the evil eye painted on her face. Perhaps she is a witch."

At first the townsfolk were alarmed by such a suggestion. But then questions surfaced. "Why doth Goody Barbie sound hollow when she is tapped? And what about those feet? A little like goats' hooves, wouldn't you say?"

But the piece of evidence that really sank Goody Barbie was the irrefutable fact that year after year she never aged.

"Ahh, a woman who escapes menstruation, childbirth, wrinkles, hot flashes, cellulite, drooping breasts and osteoporosis," the old hags mused. "Let's burn her to a crisp."

Try as they might, though, Goody Barbie would not die. They swung her from a tree, crushed her with stones, threw her to the bottom of a lake and even set her on fire. Still she smiled.

When at last a couple of ten-year-old boys got hold of her and replaced her head with one of G.I. Joe's, the townsfolk breathed a sigh of relief. Surely, they concluded, she came from the devil's workshop.

Now how could they have known about Mattel way back then?

Instructions: Who hath time to play with dolls, child! Hath the cows been milked? The butter churned? The itsy-bitsy bits of wood chips gathered for the fire? Idleness is the Devil's helpmate, you know, now be off before I take the switch to you.

Discussion Questions:

1) What are the flaws in this logic: Witches are made of wood. Wood floats. Barbies float. Barbies are therefore made of wood.

2) At Barbie's trial on witchcraft charges, prosecutors listed several accusations which they argued supported their case that Barbie was a witch. Which is the most compelling:

a) When burned, Barbie releases enough toxic fumes to kill the entire village plus its pets.

b) Her head turns 360 degrees, just like that little girl in the Exorcist movie.

c) She doesn't blink.

3) The hallucinations among townsfolk in Salem has been linked to a crop of molded rye that produced a spore whose properties, once ingested, mirrored those of lysergic acid. LSD. In light of this theory, tell us, why are the letters on this page square-dancing to the Artist Formerly Known as Prince's hit song "Kiss"?

BARBIE ANTOINETTE
AT THE FRENCH REVOLUTION

Goal: To witness the decline of the royal empire in the Age of Reason and to find a use for those extra Barbie heads left over from your brother's "acting out" phase.

What You Will Need:

Snooty Princess Barbie—Big dress, big hair, big blade, big mess.

Wussy Little French King Ken—Watch him run and run and yet he never gets away.

Mobs of angry French peasants—A smelly bunch, like to storm.

Background: If there ever were a time for Barbie to flourish, it was late 18th century France. Women didn't wear long puffy dresses just for special occasions, they wore them everyday. And hair, forget it. There were endless uses for Barbie wigs, hair extensions and even bird cages. The Barbie Hair Salon was jam packed every morning and there were balls to show off the hard hair work every night.

There was only one problem—peasants, lots of them. They were always complaining—about lack of food, lack of land and lack of control over their own natural destiny. Bitch, bitch, bitch.

Of course Barbie Antoinette, always cheerful, helpful and willing to see the bright side of things, tried to understand. When one night, during another one of those annoying famines, some peasants showed up at the palace asking for bread, Barbie Antoinette very sensibly said, "Let them eat cake." They rudely booed her instead.

"Grumpy dieters," she murmured.

One day Little Louis XVI Ken made a dreadful suggestion. He said they should dress up as peasants and flee Paris and the country which they ruled or face certain death.

"Dress up as peasants," a horrified Barbie Antoinette exclaimed. "But what will my ladies in waiting say?"

As it turned out, her ladies in waiting said "May you rest in peace" for Barbie Antoinette and Little Louis didn't make it very far before they were brought back, tried for treason and executed. Which proves that keeping your figure is a matter of mind over batter.

Instructions: March Barbie with hands tied behind back to waiting kitchen knife. Assuming favorite French accent say: "Okaaay, you aristocratic *batard,* you have one last request—eh. A Gaulloise? A chardonnay? A paté de fois gras? A rendezvous? An au revoir? When you run out of lame French phrases, yank her head off. Good for hours of rainy-day fun.

Discussion Questions:

1) Barbie has just been invited to the weekly beheading and she's the guest of honor! What cut dress looks good dancing headless on the guillotine platform—high or low?

2) The origin of the French Revolution has been the subject of much scholarly study. Some academics argue it was the outgrowth of an intellectual movement that elevated the power of the common man, others say it was merely a result of a growing peasant population faced with a shortage of goods and services. Still a few say it occurred because the state was bankrupt. Compare and contrast these ideas. And then compare and contrast Midge with Skipper. Notice any similarities. Doesn't that make you wonder sometimes?

BARBIE CURIE *New* She Glows!!

Goal: To discover the element that would lead to the most powerful method of total annihilation the world has ever known and to get two of those nifty, if perhaps a little gaudy, gold medallions that might look okay if you were invited to a really fancy party and you didn't wear any other jewelry. Except maybe a watch. Yeah, a watch would be okay. But it'd have to be a gold watch. And real gold, not some tacky...

What You Will Need:

Another French Know-It-All Barbie—Comes with oversized head to accommodate massive brain. May also use to play "Simone de Beauvoir Barbie and Ken Paul Sartre Exist to Party!"

Radium, uranium, polonium, various chemistry equipment.—Can be found at any local nuclear reactor. Just go the back door and ask for remnants.

An approving bourgeoisie—But you couldn't possibly understand because you are just some materialistic American whose capability for creativity goes no further than the rear bumper of your gas-guzzling Lincoln Towne Car!

Background: One evening, after a day of sun-fun surfing and volleyball, Barbie Curie noticed her deep tan line.

"Hmmm," she thought as she slipped into a cool-cotton, winter white sundress.

"Burning as the end result of the sun's perpetual cycle of nuclear reactions which release large amounts of high-energy gamma radiation. Wish I could get some of that in my kitchen!"

Well, Barbie Curie wasn't the type to sit around and wait for someone to make a microwave. While Ken Curie flipped burgers in the backyard, Barbie Curie slipped into the basement to do a little cooking of her own. After carefully measuring the atomic weights of polonium and radium, she bombarded them with alpha particles and, voila! Not one but two Nobel Prizes.

"Dinner's ready," Ken called down.

"In a minute," Barbie Curie yelled up as she applied a little of the uranium/polonium foundation on her face for that secret glow.

Unfortunately, Ken Curie thought Barbie Curie's concoction was just another one of her crazy margaritas, drank it, went loopy and promptly stepped out onto the street where his perfect plastic head was crushed by a horse. But that's an icky ending and not one Barbie Curie likes to think about much.

Instructions: Using Planck's equation in which the energy of the basic quantum is directly proportional to the frequency of the oscillator in which $h=6.63 \times 10^{-34}$ power, add some radium, tequila, a little triple sec, lime juice and ice in a blender. Whirrr. Salt the glass.

Discussion Questions:

1) Barbie Curie, except for her previous incarnation as Malibu Barbie Curie, always was careful of harmful rays, making sure to liberally slather on a sunblock with an SPF of at least thirty-two. Yet she eventually wasted away and went insane from long-term radiation poisoning. How was this possible?

2) Barbie Curie often has dreams that she is invited to the Nobel Prize ceremonies and that she shows up naked. Considering the modern theory that Barbie could be perceived as an anti-feminist fashion icon whose purpose is to implant into the sub-conscious of all future women that they are nothing without clothes, interpret. Not that we're giving you hints or anything.

BARBIE STEIN AND MIDGE B. TOKLAS AND THEIR PARIS SALON

Goal: To find that lost generation of Barbies your mother thinks she may have accidentally sold at last summer's yard sale.

What You Will Need:

A Barbie—is a Barbie is a Barbie.

Midge B. Toklas—Or maybe, for perspective, she's really Barbie. All we know is it's some kind of literary device.

Papa Ken—He's not gay, by the way, no matter what Barbie Stein implies.

Literary intelligentsia, creative yearnings, hair curlers, spray and color.

Background: Growing up in Allegheny, Pennsylvania before the turn of the century was not easy for Barbie Stein. She never quite felt part of the crowd. She had a funny way of speaking, for one thing.

"Hey Barbie," her friends said. "Let's go pick some flowers."

"A rose is a rose is a rose is a…" Barbie Stein replied.

"Whatever," her friends interrupted.

And while she was good at school and even thought of being a doctor at one

time, she could remember only one thing—all roads lead to Paris. Or was it Gaul. No, Gaul was divided into three parts. Anyway, before she got too confused she settled at the famous 27 Rue de Fleurs with her lover, secretary and biographer Midge B. Toklas. They immediately set upon a dream vocation—to open a Barbie Paris Salon.

"Your hair has so many angles, so many cuts," Barbie Stein remarked one day to Picasso who came in for a rinse and a set. "I think I'll call the style cubist." And so cubism was born and is still popular in some Soho salons.

"Why, Hemingway," Barbie barbed as she trimmed the famous author's whiskers. "I believe you look exactly like one of the Village People."

"That's it," said Hemingway, slamming down the *Paris Herald Tribune* and wiping off the shaving cream. "I don't know what you and Toklas do upstairs, but leave me out of it. I'm going off for a drink at the Ritz with Sherwood Anderson and then I'm off to the bullfights and after that I'm going to find the most beautiful woman …"

"Oh, stop the hissy fit," Barbie Stein said as she pushed him back in the chair. "Remarks are not literature."

And so this witty reparte continued until Barbie Stein's salon became quite famous for its stream-of-consciousness hair cuts. As for her writing, well, people smiled and politely praised her work. But after all, Barbie Stein was a Barbie, and tended to write stuff like this: "…One never discusses anything with anybody who can understand one discusses things with people who cannot understand."

So, for obvious reasons, she kept to the beauty business.

Instructions: What? Do you think this is playing? Do you think this is the most that can be done with your creative ability? Let me tell you, as long as you keep playing Barbie there is no hope for you. No hope, I say. Art is discipline; discipline is art!

Discussion Question:

Barbie Stein thinks Hemingway is over the top. Hemingway says he just wants a little taken off the top. What kind of insult should Barbie Stein lay on him to complement his beard and repressed sexuality?

BARBIE BRAUN'S WEDDING DAY

Goal: To get your man to finally pop the question, even if he's just about to pop off.

What You Will Need:

Eva Braun Barbie—Blonde, blue-eyed Barbies only please. All non-Aryan Barbies are inferior and must be discarded.

Führer Ken—Comes with only one left ball—which is more than most Kens can boast.

A bunker, a group of loyal-to-the-end cronies, Nazis—Apparently they can still be found in some parts of the military these days.

Background:

Barbie Braun was blonde, athletic and cheerful with no personal ambition, but with a few exciting jobs here and there. One might say she bore a striking resemblance to what some describe as Barbie's sleazy forerunner—the German pornographic "Lilli" doll.

Just like Barbie and Ken, Barbie Braun and Ken Führer had been dating for years. Still, Ken Führer hadn't asked Barbie Braun to marry him, no matter how many times she Luftwaffed his Zeitgeist.

Granted, her Ken was a little strange. Always checking for racial purity and blabbing on and on about *Mein Kampf*. And he did everything over the top. If she wanted to picnic in the Alps, he wanted to march over them. If she suggested a weekend in Paris; he'd occupy it. And so on. He was one anti-Semitic, angry, murderous little Führer but, hey, he was her anti-Semitic, angry, murderous little Führer.

Then one day her dream came true.

"Barbie Braun," Ken Führer announced amidst the romantic sound of bombs falling everywhere. "I am ready for the final solution."

"But where will we honeymoon," she asked, looking around the cement walls of their cozy underground bunker.

"Don't worry about that, my little liebchen," he said. "I'll take you someplace where you've never been before." And he did. For after trying out some deadly hors d'oeuvres on his favorite dog, Ken Führer suggested they liven up the wedding party with a few shots. Wouldn't you know it, one shot and it went straight to his head.

"No thanks," said Barbie Braun. "I'll stick with my favorite poison."

Which, you have to agree, definitely saves on air fare and hotel rates.

Instructions:

Achtung! So, you zink that you don't have to follow our orders, do you? Vell, ve have vays of making you play Barbie, ja? Now, schnell, schnell, schnell!

Discussion Questions:

1) Barbie Braun has been living at the Beghof with Ken Führer for several years. From a fashion perspective, should she wear white to the wedding. What suggestions can you offer for her "going away outfit" considering where she went? Hint: It's really warm there.

2) Do you think Barbie Braun carried the concept of "Standing By Your Man" a bit too far? Elaborate.

BARBIE PLATH: WHAT A GAS!

Goal: To learn about the life of a Barbie who became one of the finest feminist poets and to finally use that E-Z Bake Oven for something other than those under-cooked brownies you always make.

What You Will Need:

Perfect Poet Barbie—Search the bottom of the dumps.

A bell jar—A very excellent way to show off Barbie accessories, especially the earrings. A little too hot when the glare of society is beating down.

Background: Barbie Plath was a writer very much like her counterpart, Barbie Roberts, in a real book called "Barbie's New York Summer." In that book, Barbie Roberts was a beautiful blonde teenager who won a scholarship to intern on a big Manhattan fashion magazine. Guess what—Barbie Plath did too! And both spent a lot of time worrying about the boyfriends they left behind at home. Poor country Ken.

But unlike Barbie Roberts, Barbie Plath had a few more things on her mind. Usually little tiny metal things. And they gave a big shock. Zzzzz.

In fact you can think of Barbie Plath as a Barbie Roberts who feels as though she's got an imaginary thumb stuck right in the middle of her eyeball and it's constantly pressing on her brain. Now how do you find a hat to go with that?

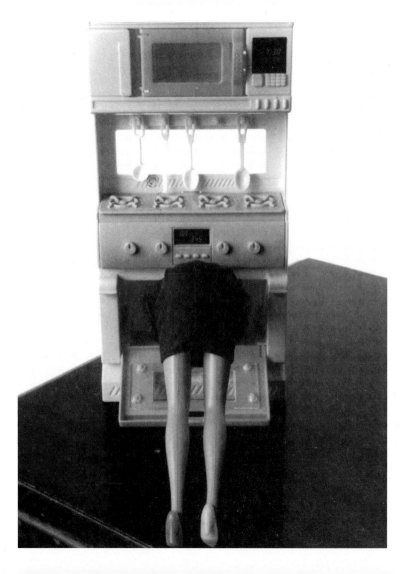

That's why Barbie Plath could write such poems as this, her most famous:

Barbby (1962)

You do not do, you do not do
Where did I put my little black shoe?
Why do I have this pointy foot
I am so white; where is my suit?

Barbby I have to kill you
Except you are already dead—
Must think of something else instead
How 'bout this pencil in your head?

And so on and so on for sixteen more cheerful stanzas. Whew, no wonder when things got a little tough for Barbie Plath she took the E-Z way out—if you know what we mean.

Instructions: You are not good enough, whatever you do it will not be as good as what Daddy expected. Daddy was great. Daddy was smart. You are nothing but a little doll who must sit by his big German boots and fetch his pipe. Shhhh! Daddy is working.

Discussion Questions:

Barbie Plath has been found holed up underneath the staircase of her Massachusetts home. What might be the cause?

a) She cannot reconcile her ingrained talent with the suffocating future demanded of young women in the post-war period.

b) The death of her overbearing father has left her confused and searching for permanent affirmation.

c) She ate a bottle-full of Percoset like they were Ju-Ju Bees.

d) It's Wednesday and Ken hasn't yet invited her out to the Saturday sock-hop.

J. EDGAR HOOVER KEN SHOPS AT THE BARBIE BOUTIQUE

Goal: Let the longest-running director of the FBI teach you the understated value of basic black—from its powerful use in mail to its seductive allure in a high-cut teddy.

What You will Need:

Earring Magic Ken—Bends at the gender.

Roy Cohn Ken—Sold only Hell.

Miniature microphones, crime lab, $1.2 billion annual allocation of federal funds, garters

Background: Poor J. Edgar Hoover Ken. As the longest-running director of the FBI he had so many important responsibilities—refilling Marilyn Monroe's prescriptions, emptying Fidel Castro's ashtrays, trampling on everyone else's civil rights. Not to mention all that filing! After updating the secret files on his secret friends and secretly double-checking the lists of his secret enemies, there was barely enough time at the end of the day to take the Hot Rod for a spin to the neighborhood soda fountain.

Thank goodness for Barbie—Barbie's Boutique that is.

Here J. Edgar Hoover Ken could relax and let out the real he...or make that she. Boas, floor-length satin kimonos, and nifty little spiked heels. His very special outfit, Barbie's "Orgy in the Plaza Hotel" ensemble, came with mini, black wig and Bible (for heightened enjoyment and eternal salvation). He loved all of Barbie's styles, except the reds, of course, and he wasn't too fond of the pinkos, either.

J. Edgar Hoover Ken didn't see the harm in a little after-hours cross-dressing with his friend, FBI assistant Clyde Tolson. As J. Edgar Hoover Ken used to like to say, what he did on his own time was his own business—as was what everyone else did on their own time, too. Ha, ha, ha. Funny, monomaniacal J. Edgar Hoover Ken.

There were those irksome Cosa Nostra thugs, though, always threatening to show secret pictures of J. Edgar Hoover Ken and fellow communist fighter Roy Cohn in compromising positions.

"There is nothing to be done about people like that except just ignore them," J. Edgar Hoover Ken said with a sigh. "God, some people can be so clothes-minded."

Top Secret Instructions: Strip Ken of all ethics, honor and humility. Blow up ego. Insulate from all reality. Arm heavily. Adjust mascara.

Discussion Questions:

1) J. Edgar Hoover Ken is going to take Cheerleading Barbie to the high school prom. Barbie plans to wear a midnight blue evening dress trimmed in black lace with matching pumps. What color purse should J. Edgar Hoover carry, provided that it is large enough to hide his Magnum Colt .45?

2) What does not belong?—Roy Cohn, the Mafia, Clyde Tolson, the investigation of James Earl Ray? (Hint: All have been under J. Edgar Hoover Ken—except for the Mafia. That's been on his back)

BANKING IS FUN WITH BARBIE HEARST

Goal: To learn how to accessorize with various artillery for an arresting effect.

What You Will Need:

Valley Girl Terrorist—Comes with rich parents, beret and nickname. AK-47 sold separately.

Those Wacky Californian Barbie and Kens—Most models outdated. Look for discontinued dolls at fire sales.

Barbie bank. Barbie sporting goods store. Barbie prison. Barbie bummed.

Background: Growing up in Beverly Hills, Barbie Hearst thought guerrillas were funny animals that lived in the zoo and that Cin, Teko and Yolanda were back-up members of the Jackson-5. How was she to know that her wealthy parents were fascist pigs or that she, a carefree college student, was an enemy of the people? Then one night in February 1974 she was thrown into the trunk of a car and taken for a drive.

"Sorority hazing," Barbie Hearst sighed. "It's the same thing every year. Why

don't they come up with something new for once?"

After spending some time in the closet and still not finding a thing to wear, Barbie Hearst began to get desperate.

Eventually Barbie Hearst was able to meet her new friends. They told her their group was called the SLA and that she could become a member if she wished.

"ATA? ATD? DU? Sigma Chi? Hmmm, I don't seem to know SLA," she said. "Wait, let me guess, you're unchartered."

The group told her that if she wanted to join she had to perform a really daring prank—a holdup of the Sunset Branch of the Hibernia Bank. At first, Barbie Hearst was unsure, but when they promised she'd be on TV she was as game as the next sorority girl.

Well, it seems colleges don't have the tolerance they used to for Greek high jinks and Barbie Hearst found herself looking at 10 to 15 years in prison.

"Be positive," she told her lawyer Flee Bailey. "At least I didn't get suspended. Boy, would my parents be pissed then."

Instructions: Steal your sister's Barbie. Tie tiny blindfold around eyes. Bind hands. Threaten to drop her into the running disposal unless your sister forks over all her accumulated allowance. When she does, drop Barbie into the disposal anyway. Say, "Oops, she slipped." Make sure to disconnect disposal before sister repeats instructions, this time substituting your left hand for Barbie.

Discussion Questions:

1) When the BLO—the Barbie Liberation Organization—switched the voice boxes of Barbies and GI Joes a few years back so that Barbie said "Eat Lead, Cobra" and Joe said "Math class is tough" the anonymous group said it was making a political statement. Mattel called it product tampering. Which is correct? By the way, what would you make Barbie say? What if you put Joe's head on Barbie's body and inserted Mickey Mouse's voice box? Hey, how about that Oliver North doll that came out a few years ago?

2) Barbie Hearst learned a lot about banking when she was with the SLA. You can learn a lot about banking too just by sending us your parents checking account number, along with copies of their social security cards. (Make sure the signatures are clear!) We'll write back from our new homes in Rio de Janeiro just as soon as we find the time.

ANITA HILL BARBIE

Goal: To get a front-row seat at the Senate confirmation hearings of a Supreme Court Justice and become the butt of stockbroker jokes nationwide.

What You Will Need:

Super Barbie—Able to leap over inflated male egos in a single bound.

Conservative African-American Supreme Court Justice Ken—Rare item. Last we checked there was only one.

A panel of white Kens—"Out-of-Touch" Ken is best.

A mob—For "high-tech" lynching.

A can of Coke, a pubic hair.

Background: Anita Hill Barbie was, like other Barbies, tall, had the perfect figure and had dates galore! She not only had a groovy job as a law professor, she had a big secret, too. Once her boss, Judge Ken Thomas, yelled, "there's a pubic hair in my Coke!" What a funny thing to say.

He also told her which clothes made her look sexy. Of course, every Barbie knows that's what clothes are for, otherwise Barbie wouldn't have so many short,

satiny, tight dresses. But even Barbie knows that while boys are supposed to notice pretty dresses, they're not allowed to talk about them (Ken never does). That's called sexual harassment and it's a violation of Barbie's civil rights.

Then Anita Hill Barbie's former boss was nominated to the U.S. Supreme Court. So Anita Hill Barbie told a group of Senators (all Kens) her secret. She thought they'd want to know.

They didn't.

Some of the Senators thought she was too much of a Barbie, despite her Yale law degree, and that she must have been daydreaming. Poor Anita Hill Barbie was lonely because she hadn't married a Ken yet, others said. She probably just got her story mixed up with a book about a devil-possessed teenage girl, said another. Such a silly girl, they concluded, she should know better than to reveal her sexual fantasies on national television.

In the end, Anita Hill Barbie went back to being a law professor and Judge Ken Thomas went to the Supreme Court, where he will remain for life. And there, like all other Kens, he sits and smiles and doesn't say anything at all. Of course, Judge Antonin Scalia does the talking for him.

Instructions:

Put Anita Hill Barbie in sensible green dress and high heels. Insert brain. Arrange Kens on dais slightly above her. Then, when Anita Hill Barbie tells the truth, pelt her with tiny rocks. See how long it takes her to crumble.

Discussion Questions:

1) Do you think if Anita Hill Barbie had chosen more modest clothing from Barbie's Great Careers line that Ken Thomas would not have been so tempted to spend valuable office time commenting on her breasts?

2) What's the point of working hard, getting a scholarship to college, a degree from a prestigious law school and a job as a law professor if, in the end, society will think of you only in terms of being a sexual object? Now do you see why Barbie skipped all that tough stuff and went straight to the sexual object part?

3) How much time do you think Judge Scalia spends playing with his Ken Thomas doll anyway? Do you suppose he can make him do other things besides writing concurring opinions?

I DON'T BAKE NO COOKIES: THE BARBIE CLINTON STORY

Goal: Try to find the real Hillary Clinton under various veneers, hairstyles and misplaced legal paperwork.

What You Will Need:

Smarter-Than-He-Is Barbie—Comes with Yale Law Degree in one hand, whip in the other.*

Wandering Eye President Ken—If lost, check the back of an Arkansas state police cruiser.

Support—For standing alone, not by your man.

Raft—For riding Whitewater.
*Note: Can get two for the price of one as Bill promised in his 1992 campaign

Background: Barbie Clinton was different from previous First Ladies. Sure, she had designer outfits, cute caps and flippy hairstyles like other Presidents' wives. (What Barbie wouldn't love that?) But Barbie Clinton—who wants you to know she's really, really smart, definitely smarter than you—also wanted to show that she

could flatten her prissy little predecessors like pancakes under a steamroller.

President Ken suggested amusing pet projects, like redesigning the Rose Garden or revamping America's healthcare system. But his second idea turned out to be too tough—even tougher than math class. Stupid hillbilly President Ken.

So Barbie Clinton decided that this time she would tackle topics she actually knew something about. No, it wasn't the law. It was how to turn $100 into $100,000 through pork bellies. It was child care. After all, Barbie Clinton had hired dozens of well-qualified people to look after her only child for most of her waking hours, so of course she knew the best way for you to raise your children, too—let other people do it!

She called the book, *It Takes A Village, Or, At Least A Thoughtfully-Landscaped Cul de Sac.*

You can imagine how popular she was after that, especially when her book sparked a nationwide trend of people dropping their kids off at the neighbors houses for weeks at a time. In fact, Barbie Clinton was such a big deal, Arkansas grand juries asked her to testify in person.

"This is awful," worried Barbie Clinton as she absentmindedly fed files into the shredder. "I don't have a thing to wear."

But thanks to Barbie's "Your Ass Is On The Line" line a Barbie is never poorly dressed—except when she doesn't have the thighs to pull off a suit in horizontal black and white stripes.

Instructions: Liberate Barbie. Douse her with intelligence, ideas and moxie. Now hang her out to dry.

Discussion Questions:

1) Barbie Clinton wore a peacock-blue flare coat and matching hat for the 1992 Inauguration. Considering her degrees from Wellesley, Yale and her vast legal experience, what color pumps did she need to wear so that she wouldn't clash with the conservative politics of the U.S. Supreme Court Justice?

2) Can you list the other times President Clinton used the phrase "Can get two for the price of one?" Hint: It's illegal in some states.

What If Barbie Were One of Us?

(Sung to the tune of "What if God Was One of Us?"
With apologies to Joan Osborne)

If Barbie were real, who would she be ?
And would she have a wrinkled face
 If you could meet with her in all her makeup?
What would you change
If you could change one feature?

Yeah, yeah, Barbie's fat
Yeah, yeah, Barbie's short
Yeah, yeah, yeah, yeah, yeah.

What if Barbie were one of us?
With wide hips, like most of us
Just a woman in a rush
Trying to make her way home.

If Barbie gained weight, what would she look like?
And would you want to see
Her in white stretch pants
And could you picture her
With things like pimples and with leg hair and some cramps?

And all those problems?

Yeah, yeah Barbie's short
Yeah, yeah, Barbie's fat
Yeah, yeah, yeah, yeah, yeah.

What if Barbie were one of us?
With wide hips, like most of us
Just a woman in a rush
Trying to make her way home
Trying to make her way home
Wishing she could be alone.
But goddamit there's the phone
If it's my boss then I'm not home.

Yeah, yeah Barbie's fat
Yeah, yeah, Barbie's short
Yeah, yeah, yeah, yeah yeah.

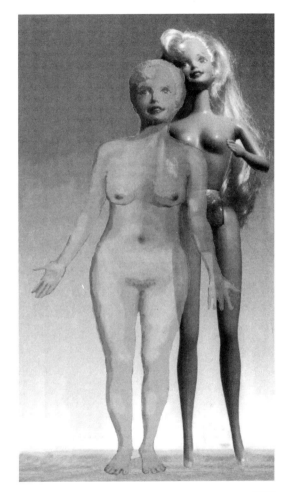

Sarah Strohmeyer is a freelance writer and newspaper reporter. She lives in Vermont with her husband and two children.

BACKSTAGE PASS: Interviews with Women in Music $16.95
by Laura Post with a foreword by Dar Williams

BACKSTAGE PASS is a joy for any music lover—a terrific collection of intimate, behind-the-scenes chats with today's most talented women singers, songwriters and musicians.
In this lively book Laura Post provides a comprehensive collection of interviews with forty vibrant women musicians. In an industry characterized by corporate packaging and glitzy promotion, these women have distinguished themselves as independent and assertive voices.

TALES FROM THE DYKE SIDE Humorous Essays by Jorjet Harper $10.95

A unique blend of humor and wry commentary. Through side-splitting spoofs, reports from the front, and real-life stories that demonstrate what it's like to be a lesbian in our changing times, Tales from the Dyke Side contains some of the quirkiest commentary you'll ever read.

Jorjet Harper is smart, hilarious and seriously depraved. –Alison Bechdel

OFF THE RAG, Lesbians Writing on Menopause $12.95
Edited by Lee Lynch and Akia Woods

Among the many women contributing to this anthology are some of the most well-known and well-read lesbian writers of our time—Sarah Dreher, Sally Gearhart, Karla Jay, Merrill Mushroom, Joan Nestle, Terri de la Peña, and Valerie Taylor. They have influenced our reading and thinking over the years and now offer us a particularly powerful view of their changing lives.

I CHANGE, I CHANGE Poems by Barbara Deming $12.95
Edited and with a forward by Judith McDaniel Preface by Grace Paley

Barbara Deming was one of the most dearly loved and respected political activists and essayists of our time. *I Change, I Change* is a collection of previously unpublished poems, collected by Barbara shortly before her death. These poems give fresh insight into her personal passions and the overwhelming importance of love in her life.